Whatever Happened to the **Pecords?**

The True, Unsolved Mystery of Two Families Who Vanished Simultaneously in Fall, 1959

James P. Naughton

Key Publishing Company

ISBN 978-09858377-0-9

Whatever Happened to the Pecords?

Copyright 2013 by James P. Naughton

Key Publishing Company
www.KeyPublishingCompany.com

51 Gosnold Road
North Kingstown, RI 02852
401-885-1838
jnaughton43@cox.net

Printed in the U.S.A.

Editing, design, and layout by
Martha Nichols/aMuse Productions®

I dedicate this story to all my
childhood friends who have passed on, including
Ricky Dickman, who left us way too young;
Doug Sweet, who passed earlier this year; and
Tony Marchese, a blonde-haired, blue-eyed
Italian kid whom everyone liked
and who also passed away too young.

≻···≺

Acknowledgments

First of all, I want to acknowledge and thank my parents, James and Julia Naughton, who had the unimaginable courage to leave their families in Ireland and immigrate here to America, the place that my dad always referred to as the "greatest country on earth." I would also like to thank Pratt & Whitney, famous manufacturer of jet engines, for giving them jobs and a new life in my hometown of East Hartford, Connecticut. This allowed for my sister Kathleen and me to also have unlimited opportunities in our great country. I am also sure that my parents were all smiles in heaven, when their grandson, my sister Kathleen's son and my nephew, Sean Connolly, and his wife, Carol Connolly, joined Pratt & Whitney's legal department as attorneys so many years after their parents retired from the company.

I also extend sincere thanks to Todd Andrews, Vice President (College Relations and Advancement) and his staff at Goodwin College (Riverside Drive, East Hartford, Connecticut) for extending a hand to help me in my desire to produce this book. I discuss the significance of Goodwin College and the information they provided to me as I was doing research for the book in my hometown.

To John Choquette: We became close friends toward the end of high school, and while he wasn't a buddy in the story, John, in addition to being a great friend, provided me with a lot of direction and invaluable information for my book research, including special access to the town library, the police department, and help locating many historic real estate documents and maps. He was the one who put together the valuable connection between me and Todd Andrews and Lee Sawyer at Goodwin College. John has worked in local government since we both graduated from Central Connecticut University in the early seventies. A tireless worker, he has spent the last 20 years in various positions within our hometown of East Hartford including Assistant to the Mayor under several administrations and Director of Development. Most recently John was once again promoted to the position of Assistant to the Mayor.

To my childhood friend of the south end and former Willowbrook Grammar School alumnus, Bill (Billy) White, and my north end friend from St. Mary's, Jim (Jimmy) Maloney—a big *thanks* for helping me remember the "good old days." I hope we will continue to meet up occasionally to celebrate, reminisce, and laugh about a shared bygone era over a few cold ones.

Special thanks to my high school English teacher, Mr. Engle. He believed in me at a time when I didn't believe in myself. I can still hear him cry "*NOOoooo!*" after telling him that I had quit the college curriculum and was considering dropping out of school completely. They say that, when one looks back, they can often recall someone—a coach, a family member, or, as in my case, a teacher—who really had your back. Thank you!

Thanks also to my designer, Martha Nichols, at aMuse Productions® for the design, layout, and editing feedback of my book. Martha also made my book's cover.

Finally, to my family: my wife Sharon; my elder son Timothy and his wife Cristina and our grandchildren, Jack, Sam, and Cole; as well as my middle son Mathew and my daughter Erin. Thanks for believing in me, inspiring me, and pushing me to share my stories.

The reader should be aware that I, like all authors, used some "literary license" while discussing some of my memories. One of my goals in addition to discussing the missing family was to give the reader a view, a perspective into the fifties. You might note that some of my flashbacks were of events that occurred a little before 1959 and some actually took place a year or two afterward. It seemed convenient for the flow and continuity of the story. I hope you agree.

Prologue

I am convinced that my tale of a true-life mystery was enabled by the decade of the 1950s—so convinced that I decide to include a number of details as evidence.

By the end of the fifties, the world had largely recovered from World War II, and the cold war was evolving. Besides the advent of television, Paper-Mate developed the first ball point pen. The Chevrolet Corvette became the first car to have an all fiberglass body. Jonas Salk invented the polio vaccine, the Russians put up the Sputnik, the first satellite to orbit the earth, and Ray Croc mass-produced the American hamburger and started the monster McDonald's chain. The era of the fifties in the view of many, had an immeasurable impact on my fellow Baby Boomers. (Wikipedia "borrowed" some of this.) It was an exciting time that portended change.

As is true of many eras, there were many signs, not always apparent to everyone at the time, which were telling us change was coming and that we would play a major role. When we read the Dick Tracy daily comic strips and saw him speaking into a radio wristwatch, we wondered to ourselves, "Was this ever going to really be possible to do?" Even the cars started sprouting fins in the rear of their bodies. They began taking on the look of a rocket. Looking back, I think they were signaling that we were going to put a man on the moon. A few years later, Detroit produced "the Comet," which was my family's first automobile.

Earlier in the decade we listened to radio and tried to imagine what it was like to travel with Sergeant Preston of the Mounties and his sled dog, Yukon King, as they chased the bad guys during the Canadian Northwest Gold Rush. On the radio, we could hear the sounds of the wind (*brrrr...swish, swish, crash!!!!*) and snow blowing and the mushing of dogs (*bark, bark, growls, howls*). However, because we couldn't yet see these skits, our imaginations continued to expand all the way to northern Canada.

There were many positive consequences of not having a TV until the mid- to late-fifties (for many) or having few organized sports other than Little League. It forced us to be creative and invent new games and fun. We were allowed time to develop expansive imaginations and be ingenious.

This contributed to great change and many inventions later on. In his book, *The Fifties*, David Halberstam regarded the fifties as "seminal" in determining what our country is today. It caused many of us to become adventurers and eventually entrepreneurs. Sure we did crazy "kid" things while developing our minds, but we also learned the meaning of true friendships. We swore oaths and kept them. We borrowed a tradition from the Indians and cut our hands just enough so that after joining wounds with our buddies, we became "blood brothers" for life. In addition, for many, the evolution of "rock 'n' roll" brought us a type of relief from the "rigors" of our young teenage lives. I use the term evolution, but it was more like a revolution in music history. The number of "oldies" we hear today, playing as part of modern-day commercials more than 50 years later, is amazing!

> *Stay, ahhh,*
> *Just a little bit longer*
> *Please, please, please, please,*
> *Tell me that you're going to.*

That great song ("Stay"), performed by Maurice Williams and the Zodiacs, was written by Williams in the fifties and debuted in 1960.

When my family finally got our first TV, it was probably one of the most exciting time of my teenage life. I can still hear the "William Tell Overture" introducing The Lone Ranger as the masked man galloped up a hill on his horse Silver, yelling "Hi yo Silver—away!!" His companion, a generic Indian named Tonto, called the Ranger "Kemo Sabe." We heard it on radio, but now we listened and watched in our living rooms. Our lives were changed forever. And silently our creative thinking time began to be taken from us.

During the fifties, we played outside from the dawn of day till dark, stopping only for a quick lunch and dinner. Our summers gave us the opportunity to run thru water sprinklers, to play neighborhood softball games, hide and seek, red rover come over, and other games we would invent ourselves. We went to the beach, a lake, or a pond and listened to some corny songs a year later on our transistor radios: "It Was an Itsy Bitsy, Teenie Weenie, Yellow Polka Dot Bikini" (by Bryan Hyland, written 1959 and released in 1960). With all this simple playing, we ended up with many friends and we learned to have each other's back—that is, be *real* buddies. In my end of town, we were in close proximity to the rivers and the woods. Thus, we made rafts, tree swings, underground forts, played army, hunted, and fished. Looking back it seems like we never stopped.

The era, while it differed by region, city, and county, overall, it provided most of us with comparable experiences. Certainly the rock 'n' roll music revolution tied the rural residents and city dwellers with its unique tunes, now referred to as "oldies." When a teenaged boy heard Elvis belting out "Don't Be Cruel" and "All Shook Up," regardless of where he lived, he grabbed a broomstick or baseball bat in lieu of a guitar and started singing along; some would even shake their hips and knees imitating "the King."

Whatever Happened to the Pecords? has similarities to the movie "Stand by Me" that include the era, teenagers coming of age, and a mystery—not of a body but of a whole family who vanished one Friday evening. In contrast, this story is true, and its main character is yours truly, the author.

As a result of sharing my teenage mystery story of 1959, my hope is to provide my readers with a more intimate understanding of what the time was like. The setting is the blue-collar town of East Hartford, made famous by Pratt & Whitney, manufacturer of jet engines. In addition to the book's core mystery story, you will be provided with a number of "flashbacks" that I experienced during events of 1959 that will give you a window to peer into and see life as it was in the fifties thru the eyes of a teenager "coming of age."

≻···≺

As I reached the top of the embankment, I began pulling the vines off my feet, simultaneously lifting my head upward. I thought I caught a glint of light on something metallic to my left. My mind instantly registered "car," and I realized incredulously that it was covered with branches. Camouflaged! I thought. I also saw two people in the front seat—the shadows concealed their faces.

I was stunned, but I don't think it was noticeable—at least, I hoped it wasn't. "Hide!" I whispered urgently back to my friends from the corner of my mouth. I nonchalantly turned to my right, and instead of heading toward the abandoned house, I began quick-stepping toward the trail heading into the woods. I heard a door slam. Many thoughts were racing through my mind. I didn't have time to grasp what was happening. I just had a sick feeling in my stomach that it wasn't good.

I am going to break part of a childhood "Stand By Me"* oath. I will attempt to provide you with as much information as I can recall regarding a real-life mystery from the late nineteen-fifties. It's the story of a shocking experience I had while making my Friday evening collections on my Hartford Times newspaper route. A customer—actually two families—disappeared: gone forever, as far as anyone could determine.

---

*   A 1986 buddy movie about a coming-of-age experience involving four teenage misfits.

I thought I saw two men, one wearing a fedora hat and the other smoking a cigarette. Initially, I didn't want to give the impression that I saw anything; instead, I wanted them to think I was just taking my Red Ryder BB gun for a casual romp in the woods. However, when I heard the car door slam, I knew two things: I wanted to protect my buddies—from what, I didn't know; just instinct—and I had to disappear in the woods—fast!

I was being chased but I wasn't panicking because of my youthful stamina and familiarity with the forest and surrounding area. However, after about 10 minutes or so, I began thinking of my family and flashbacks of my young teenage life darted in and out of my mind.

>⋯<

My hometown of East Hartford, Connecticut, is headquarters for United Technologies Corporation. I remember it as Pratt & Whitney—P & W, creator of the best jet engines in the world. Pratt & Whitney ran three round-the-clock shifts for 36,000 employees during the fifties and early sixties.

Pratt & Whitney Aircraft main administration building.

You might say it made the town, and in fact, it did: East Hartford, Connecticut, was a factory town—blue collar personified.

We weren't old enough to comprehend its significance or its importance to our families' livelihoods. All we knew was that our fathers went there for work—the morning shift began at 7 A.M. and ended at 3:30 P.M.; the second shift began at 3:30 P.M. and ended at 12:00 A.M.; and the 12 A.M. shift ended at 7 A.M., 5 days a week. It seemed like everyone's father—and often, as in my family's household, our mothers—worked there. Pratt & Whitney dominated just about everything in our lives.

Pratt & Whitney Aircraft emblem located at entrance to the main administration building.

So much has been written of the nineteen fifties. The fifties are now a part of our past and ingrained in our culture. Most Baby Boomers recall Walt Disney's Mickey Mouse Club and its serialization of "The Adventures of Spin and Marty." I later also loved "Stand By Me," the 1980s movie set in the 1950s, and countless other stories that were set in the fifties.

I don't know if the world needs another "fifties" story, but I have been wanting to get this one off my chest for some time. I leave it for my grandchildren, and I hope and pray they don't inherit their grandfather's Huckleberry Finn–crazy-adventurist ways.

If you are a Baby Boomer or older, you probably won't need much background, but for others who might read this tale, it should be helpful.

The era is my pre-public high school period in the late fifties.... East Hartford was somewhat famous, as it was (and is) home to the world's greatest jet engine manufacturer, Pratt & Whitney. The town is separated from the Connecticut capital city Hartford by the Connecticut River, where I spent much of my free time in my pre- and early teens.

≻ · · · ≺

I dove into a gully and began belly crawling. There was a huge oak tree on my left, a tiny hint of autumn color on its leaves, so I crawled behind it unseen, or so I hoped. The two men went flying past me, and I began to feel relieved. Unfortunately, fear took hold, and I was aware of feeling mentally stuck there, and my body was pretty much frozen even though it was a warm early fall evening. I was also amazed at how fast a couple of older guys could run. Thank goodness, they were gone, and I sat and caught my breath.

✂ · · · ✂

The Texaco gas station in town had attendants who wore uniforms with police-style eight-point hats. They also had a metal, five-foot-tall, red Coca Cola machine out front. For a nickel, you got a glass bottle of the most delicious, refreshing drink ever. Why did it taste so much better back then? Was there really a tinge of "coke" in the Coke? Whatever the reason, it's never tasted as good since. It tasted even better at the soda fountains when the soda jerks added vanilla, cherry, or chocolate extract.

Of course, in the south end where I grew up, Pratt & Whitney Aircraft (United Technologies Corporation)

Main Street, East Hartford.

and its buildings seemed to sprawl just about everywhere you looked. Main Street hosted such stores as Sage Allen, Harmacs Men's Store, Maxwell Drug Store, First National Super Market, and Neil's Sporting Goods store. The most pronounced landmark was the large white Congregational church with its clock steeple. The area was known as "church corners" and was the main bus stop in town. From this site, one could look across Main Street and view the public library, the fire department, and the East Hartford Town Hall. Further south, you would find the A&P Super Market and Marques's neighborhood grocery store. Richard Marques had attended St. Mary's a year ahead of us.

The Eastwood Theater was also in the center of town. Here, you would find me and my friends every Saturday afternoon for the matinee; for years we watched

Church Corners, center of East Hartford.

the latest Disney cartoons, John Wayne, the Three Stooges, Tarzan, and many more.

Surprisingly, I can't recall many restaurants in town other than DiLeo's, whose owner's kids, Peggy and Jimmy, attended St. Mary's parochial school around the same time I did. I say *surprisingly* because, after all, we lived in a town that hosted the largest jet engine manufacturer in the world, and it was a time of nearly full employment.

I believe town residents simply lived frugally. Many were children and grandchildren of immigrants and the Great Depression era and were determined to become financially independent, so they ate at home most of the time and put their savings into the banks or the Aircraft Federal Credit Union. The Connecticut Bus Company provided transportation all over town and into the capital city of Hartford and the many surrounding towns and villages. As a result, most residents did not feel the need to own an automobile.

One the most popular eateries was the Triple A Diner, where my friends and I got into trouble when a couple of pious church ladies pointed at us, recklessly sitting in one of the diner's 4' x 8' windows that faced Main Street, enjoying a turkey club on a Friday (remember "no meat on Friday"?). Not good, particularly when one is attending Catholic school.

Of course, on the east side of town near the project, Mayberry Village had the Marco Polo Italian Restaurant, where we went after dances for pizza and Coke as we grew older. That was it for restaurants in what was at the time considered a boom town.

Another highlight in the north end was Macchi's Shoe Repair Shop. There was something mesmerizing about the smells of leather and shoe polish. Of course, most middle-class parents of the era didn't rush out and buy you brand new shoes every six months—instead, you went to Macchi's and had the old ones repaired.

Whatever Happened to the Pecords?

The Triple A Diner on North Main Street.

Watching someone repairing a shoe was fascinating to us kids and more money for the family savings accounts. Our other favorite north-end spot was near St. Mary's: Prospect Drug Store and its soda fountain.

Marco Polo Restaurant, popular after-dance eating spot.

Other than these landmarks, our north-end lives revolved around St. Mary's church and school. St. Mary's School was a huge brown brick building that could have passed for a small high school. For some of us, the convent, where we often cleaned the barrels and other janitorial-type jobs for the sisters, was a viable alternative to what you may know as detention.

≻···≺

I also remember how Sahara-like the summers were back then. They were brutally hot. The houses in the United Homes Housing Project consisted of plywood construction with no insulation, no air conditioning, and maybe one fan if you were lucky. I tell my skeptical children that I used to lie in bed—our parents made us come inside and go to bed by 8:30!—and feel so uncomfortable I couldn't sleep. It was at least

Whatever Happened to the Pecords? 11

Above: *Front entrance of St. Mary's School, founded in the 1800s.*
Below: *St. Mary's School is now an apartment complex.*

Opposite: *St. Mary's Sisters of Mercy convent; it later became the Benjamin Callahan Funeral Home.*

85° inside the house, with no air moving. I would lie there perspiring, listening to the older kids play a game of softball under the lights at the project's ball field. I sometimes snuck out of our first-floor bedroom window to watch the excitement and maybe catch a breeze.

The greatest thing about summer and the project was that there were probably at least 20 kids around my age, so we were always inventing games, making sling shots, shooting homemade bows and arrows, and riding our bikes. Once in a while someone would turn on a sprinkler for us to run through, but that was rare. A few families had automobiles and occasionally would drive everyone to a nearby lake. It was during this time that a historic (to us) song arrived: "Itsy Bitsy Teeny Weenie Yellow Polka-Dot Bikini." A little corny? Oh, yeah! But also, it was "Happy Days"—a time of innocence—and we realized it only after it was gone.

Once in a while we were able to take a bus to Martin Park, which I considered north end, although it was more in the middle-east section of town. It boasted the town's first swimming pool of the era and the best Fourth of July fireworks. As hot as the summers were in the fifties, the winters were equally cold.

There was always a foot or two of snow on the ground from December through February and early March.

As I think about it, the south end where I lived really didn't have a lot for kids back then. There were tons of bars for the Pratt & Whitney workers, which did us kids no good, although they did offer our fathers some relief from the hard factory work and the extremely hot summers.

We did have the best drive-in hamburger stand in the country: Augie and Ray's. I swear the Beach Boys song "Fun, Fun, Fun (Till Her Daddy Takes the T-Bird Away)" was written about a dark-haired beauty from Glastonbury, Connecticut. She would pull up and sit in a metallic blue '55 T-Bird and meet up with a guy from town who was a laborer a couple years older than my friends and I. We would all gape through Augie's huge windows with a tinge of jealously and sip on our shakes. The rumor was that, like the line in the song, her father found out and took away the T-Bird and that the guy turned to heavy booze for a long time.

Because I choose not to mention his name, you're probably thinking it's a stretch, but I believe it got into the song. In fact, another song, "Mustang Sally," seemed to be written about a lone girl I always saw in a nurse's uniform frequently driving her red Mustang convertible through Augie's parking lot looking for

Martin Park.

Willow Brook Elementary School, located near Pratt and Whitney Aircraft and now Goodwin College. Most of my fifties friends attended grammar school here while I traveled to St. Mary's in the north end.

someone, something; her name was, coincidentally, Sally. So it seems that Augie's not only provided the best hot dogs, hamburgers, and shakes, but it also possibly spawned a few fifties hit tunes.

Augie and Ray's Drive-In Restaurant. Established in 1946, they were famous for their hot dogs, hamburgers, and milkshakes. It is located near Pratt & Whitney Aircraft on Main Street in the South End.

Hugging the dirt and remaining as quiet as possible, for inexplicable reasons, my grammar school came to mind. I attended St. Mary's, which had a 9th grade. There, we were taught by the Sisters of Mercy, although they didn't always show it. Mercy, I mean. (Just kidding.)

≻ · · · ≺

Attending St. Mary's allowed me to have two sets of friends —the kids from St. Mary's on the north end where I attended school and the kids from the south end where I lived. There was always mischief, north or south. St. Mary's, unlike other Catholic schools, allowed us to wear street clothes instead of uniforms, probably because that's all our parents could afford. They also allowed us a two-hour lunch, I guess so the local kids could go home if they wished. I brought the same lunch every day: peanut butter and jelly and a flask of chocolate milk. If you're a middle to early Baby Boomer, you might relate to this.

Two of my north end Stand by Me buddies were Frankie Grandi and Jimmy Maloney. We decided we desperately needed fashionable haircuts, and we knew about a secret opening in the chain link schoolyard fence that was supposed to safely contain us during lunch time. Of course, we only used it on special occasions. This was one of those, and after downing our sandwiches, we headed through the fence to Gino's Barber Shop.

We decided we wanted the latest haircuts that were appearing in magazines at the time called "Flat Top Boogies" or "Chicagos." We just wanted to look cool. This haircut meant that the hair on top of your head was cut short—like a crew cut with a little spit curl in front. The sides were left long so that with the help of Pomade or Vaseline, you could comb it back into what was called a "duck's ass" or a "DA."

As we were leaving the barbershop, Gino turned up the volume on his radio as a new song debuted: "(Come Along and Be My) Party Doll," by Buddy Knox. We stood in his hallway and shuffled our feet and snapped our fingers just as Fonzie would later do on "Happy Days."

Forty minutes later, we came back looking like the coolest of the cool. Unfortunately, the sisters didn't see it that way and promptly called our parents. Keep in mind that many of our parents were from the old country, like my folks, and many were first-generation Irish, Polish, Italian, etc. East Hartford in the 1950s was literally a melting pot that seemed to work.

Frankie's mother was the first to arrive. Mine were farther away, and we didn't have a car yet.

Jimmy's parents were at work at the First National Food Company. Within seconds, Frankie's Chicago was reduced to a butch by his mother's own scissors while the sisters looked on approvingly. My mother was waiting at the bus stop and, noting the long scissors, I proceeded to run, only to be stopped by a fence. I, too, ended up with a butch.

≻···≺

Fortunately, it appeared that my buddies had heeded my warning and were safely on their way home. Now I was sorry I had even told them about discovering that the Pecord family was missing.

≻···≺

At the United Homes Housing Project, we were always inventing new games. Our parents were strict, but they didn't seem to fear us being in the surrounding woods. As a result, we all knew the woods and the Connecticut and Hockanum rivers like Huckleberry Finn knew the Mississippi. This knowledge would prove to be a lifesaver for me, as you will find out as you read about the missing family, the Pecords.

One of these new games almost ended it for yours truly. We set up a race to see who could climb to the top of a tree the fastest. In one section of the project, an amesite (an asphaltlike substance) sidewalk ran between two twenty-foot maple trees (the amesite was new due to the fact that in earlier years, the sidewalks were all wooden because the oil that was needed to make the amesite had to be saved for the war effort).

The first two in the race were my friend Billy Griffin and me. A cap gun was used as the starting pistol. I flew up the tree like a monkey and raced to the top first, only I had forgotten how fragile the top of the tree actually was. It snapped, and I fell straight down head first and landed in the soft grass only about six inches from the sidewalk! Luckily, the lower branches softened my fall a bit, but I still hit hard.

I couldn't breathe for what seemed like an eternity. My head and neck felt pushed down inside my body cavity. Finally, I started breathing again. At that age, you really don't comprehend that you could have died or been a paraplegic the rest of your life.

I seemed to be physically okay, but I began to have visions, sometimes in our apartment, sometimes outside. The visions seemed to be of a "paranormal" nature (although that word was not yet in my simple vocabulary back then), but I did talk to the visions.

I also seemed to be able to do weird stuff. One time, I bet about 12 friends that I could make a car move forward with my mind. Everyone agreed to a nickel, so I closed

United Homes Housing project* where I lived from birth until 1956. The tall chimney in the distance belonged to the Coca Cola Bottling Company.

my eyes, clenched my teeth and fists, and mentally commanded the car to move. It did. I can still remember thinking, "Holy smokes! It actually lurched forward!" Everyone scattered, and I not only didn't collect any nickels, but also it seemed like the kids were afraid of me for awhile after that.

My head still hurt every so often. I think the climax of the whole incident occurred one Friday night, after getting home from a big pre-Gillette TV Friday Night Fights

---

* *I have herein (and in many other articles I have written) included pictures of the United Homes Project, mainly because there isn't any record of its existence. It was located on Main Street in the south end of town. The current Coca Cola Bottling Company recently expanded its buildings onto the project's original site.*

bonfire and hot dogs at Chris Jamo's. (My friend Cristo and his family moved to Mayberry Village, a more upscale project, soon after.) My father turned on our television, an oval 8-inch Emerson with a "rabbit ears" antenna, so it could warm up.

For some inexplicable reason, I started telling everyone that I liked fires. I went on and on about how great fires were. Everyone told me to stop it, that I would be sorry, which made me keep going. Of course, I was really just being a kid and fooling around—or maybe it was a psychic premonition…?

Because early the next morning, my sister and I were carried from our house by a big burly fireman. I will never forget the look of sadness on my mother's face.

As it turned out, my father had placed a cigarette on the sink as he was shaving while getting ready for work early that morning. The fireman believed that when Dad picked it up, he accidentally brushed it against a towel, which slowly began to burn. It was a miracle that my mother woke up after he left and smelled smoke seeping into their bedroom. Our door (my sister and I shared a room) was closed tight, and the very thick smoke was temporarily stalled by the door, just waiting for its entry. It was later revealed that it would have blasted through in about 5 or 6 minutes more. (I don't believe in testing

Fate, but after falling 20 feet and landing on my head 6 inches from a sidewalk, plus many other close calls, I think I was meant to experience and tell this story.)

That day, compassionate neighbors took my sister and me to see the Saturday movie matinee at the Eastwood Theatre—"Sampson and Delilah." Biblical.

As I look back, it seems that everyone in the project looked out for one another. I remember when Freddie Peppin was hit by a car. Both his legs were broken. My mother organized a group of neighbors to canvass the project collecting nickels, dimes, and quarters to help with his expenses. He recuperated in his apartment, not in a hospital. That was health care, East Hartford project-style. Years later, Freddie ended up becoming a Hartford policeman, so I assume his legs healed successfully.

The damage to our home was mostly from smoke, and I promised to never say "I like fires" again!

≻…≺

Eventually, my headaches left and the visions stopped.

My folks worked hard and saved their money, and in 1956, they bought our first home. It was on Colt Street, almost directly across from Pratt & Whitney's main administrative office. The Pratt & Whitney Aircraft Federal Credit Union was on the corner of Colt and Main streets, and I ended up working there most of my high school years.

The move to Colt Street also came with a *Hartford Times* evening newspaper route for me. It was on this paper route that I met the Pecords.

The Pecords seemed like nice elderly couple. I also remember them as being stubborn—they'd had to be forced to evacuate by firemen in a motor boat during Hurricane Carol a few years earlier. Colt Street was named after Samuel Colt, from the Colt Firearms Factory. Colt decided to move with his family and senior executives across the Connecticut River from his factory, and he set up his own ferry service with his private landing at the bottom of Colt Street. I believe the Pecords lived in one of Colt's original houses or at least on one of his sites.

Hearing nothing except for some crows cawing out in the distance, and noting the setting sun, I decided to take a chance and make a beeline for the Hockanum and the rope. I thought the darkness of night would help me, but I still needed to see my way through the thick woods and brush. With my Red Ryder strapped to my shoulder and my knee aching, I began to run as fast as I could under the circumstances.

I had been thinking as I flew through the forest about how my group of south-end "Stand By Me" buddies (which is how I now refer to them because of our oath and the similarity to the movie) started to form and some of the crazy stunts we pulled. It was an era of imagination, feeling invincible in our own little teenage fifties world.

≻ · · · ≺

My next-door neighbor, Doug Sweet, was about a year older than I was. I thought of Doug as 13 going on 18 while I was 12 going on 10. Doug was a handsome boy, and all the girls liked him, especially Barbara. In addition to baseball and football games, Doug and I seemed to get into a lot of mischief.

One afternoon, we took our brand new peashooters with us to try them out. We took aim at a car waiting to turn into Pratt & Whitney for the second shift. A bunch of dried peas entered the open window. Not good! The athletic-looking driver slammed on his brakes,

Colt Street, looking west. We moved here in 1956, and it became a significant part of my Hartford Times *paper route. The street became a dirt road and was referred to as the Colt Street Extension, which ended at the Connecticut River. Colt Street was named in honor of Samuel Colt founder of Colt Firearms. Samuel Colt moved there and set up homes and a ferry service for himself and some executives.*

120 Colt Street, formerly the Pecord's house. Sitting close to the river, it was the last stop on my paper route.

opened his car door, and gave chase. No way could he catch us; we knew the lay of land better than anyone.

Unfortunately for us, he must have been an Olympic runner, because we got caught on the side of a hill heading down toward Willow Brook. Willow Brook flowed from the factory to the Hockanum River and finally into the Connecticut River. It ended up with us being dragged unceremoniously back to his car to apologize to his passengers, including his wife. I felt sick and stupid, and we were very lucky he didn't beat us to a pulp. The thought had struck me as I ran from him that maybe this was "payback" for all our pranks.

After that, we limited our "criminal" antics to shooting out streetlights with our Red Ryder BB guns. In winter, we would practice our shooting prowess in my cellar with empty paper milk cartons for targets. It wasn't until late that spring when my father was putting up the 4' x 8' screens on our sun porch that my folks realized—from the number of flies and other bugs that made their unwelcome way inside through those screens—that our many BB shots had pierced the screens stored behind our targets at the rear end of our cellar. The forfeiting of my rifle *and* my newspaper money was a small part of the punishment.

>····<

I must have run a hundred yards, jumping bushes, dodging prickers and thick branches. I had to rest. I heard nothing from my pursuers, thank God!

It's crazy, but thoughts of my paper route, my customers, neighborhood, neighbors, and my small, cozy world flashed through my head as I gasped for air. I learned later on that quite often when one is in a life-threatening situation—such as drowning—their nerves force them to think of something other than the impending disaster.

Next to Doug's house lived the Tranis. Joanie Trani and her friend Bunny Bavier also became our girlfriends—not like romantic girlfriends, though, at least not on their part! But when there was a softball game or even touch football, they were included along with my sister Kathy. Their parents became my paper route customers, also.

Soon after starting my paper route, I met a black family—only the word *colored* was used back then—who lived midway down on my street. Mrs. Carter would invite me in on collection night for some pastry. She worked at the Sage Allen Bakery in Hartford, which was probably the best pastry shop in Connecticut. The Carters became my best and favorite customers. I had never actually met and spoken to a black family until then.

Following them, I met the Frechette family who, like many of my customers, had moved from Maine for a job at P & W. In their case, they moved from Biddeford, Maine. They had two cute daughters: Rachel was a little younger than me, and she had a still-younger sister whose name I can't recall.

Sandy beach area along the Connecticut River heading north. This is one of a few beaches that I was able to navigate as I made my way north. These beaches made it possible for me to escape back home.

Rachel became a friend. I remember someone at her house had an old-fashioned recorder with a reel-to-reel setup that was about 8" tall by approximately 18" long and weighed about 4 pounds (a bit bigger than my current 2" x 4" iPod). It played "Sherry Baby" by Frankie Valli and the Four Seasons on summer nights. Even now, when I hear "Sherry Baby," I immediately associate it with summer and fun.

From Rachel's house, my next paper route stop was at Mary Ann Dobbins's house. My father was a friend of her dad's, who was a guard at Pratt & Whitney. (I later met Mary Ann at a business convention in Boston sometime in 1987. She had married Mike Russell, an executive and super talented marketing executive for a large mutual fund company and a great, personable guy.) I sheepishly apologized for pulling on her pigtails when we were kids. Of course, the Dobbinses became another *Hartford Times* customer. It seemed like everyone worked for Pratt & Whitney, and in fact, most in the neighborhood did.

Coming around the corner of Crosby Street (which was on my paper route) came Ricky Dickman carrying one of the first transistor radios that I had seen, playing "I wonder, wonder, who ba ba dooo who…*(bop!)*…Who Wrote the Book of Love?"

Ricky, after first trying to pick a fight with me, had become one of my close friends. He probably could have kicked my butt, as he was muscular and naturally strong. He ended up playing varsity football in high school for a while. That first day I was able to get him to back off after I mentioned working on my (fictional) black belt. Oh well, it worked.

When people ask me I how I remember all this stuff, I say I'm not sure, because sometimes I can't remember what I did last week. But I believe it was the fifties music that I loved (and still do) and my association of songs to events. The Dale Carnegie course on communication teaches you to associate items with many objects to help you implant them in your memory. For me, it seems to be the music.

Through all these new friends, I was introduced to King's Court project. While it wasn't exactly on my paper route, this project bordered it. It was loaded with tons of kids my age. It reminded me of United Homes, but these apartment buildings were a step up, made of brick and nicely landscaped with ball fields in the center. In fall, we played sandlot tackle football almost every night.

There was a tenant named Demarco who would sneak out and sit in his car, which faced the north end of the field. He seemed to live for the moment one of us would accidentally kick or throw a football into his yard. He would turn his bright lights on and blow his horn and rush to try and confiscate the football. It was as if he felt left out and secretly wanted to play, too. You would have felt sorry for him on Halloween night. It probably took him a week to clean everything up.

Billy White and I were visiting the Borden brothers' family apartment in King's Court when Roger handed me a rifle while his 12-year-old sister Noel (who looked like a model) stood next to me as I aimed and simulated firing it toward Bill White in a joking manner. Bill and I both wanted to ask Noel for a date but felt she was too young. Then we learned she was dating Sandy MacDougal, also of King's Court and a couple of years older than we were! And not that good-looking, either.

Ball field at King's Court project.

Bill took the rifle and pointed it in our direction. Do kids do dumb things? Yep, stupid dumb things. Roger's older stepbrother, whose name I can't recall, then took the rifle outside, cocked it, and fired it into the air. Bill and I almost fainted. We had assumed it wasn't loaded. (Bill and I still discuss this near-catastrophe every time we meet for a beer.)

King's Court was home to a large number of teenage guys and girls. There was always something going on. Regardless of whether it was a party or a ball game, we always had a fun time.

My first birthday party invitation at 13 was at King's Court at Bob Quesnette's family's apartment. I was introduced to a game I liked called "Spin the Bottle," and my first spin went to Rachel Frechette; it was only the second or third time I had kissed a girl in my young life. Ricky Dickman, however, didn't waste any time at the party and asked Rachel to go steady—and she said yes. They were married soon after high school graduation.

Remember, I was 14 going on 11, as opposed to some of my friends who were 14 were going on 18. I was a very young 14, slightly naïve in my thinking and behavior. My real first love, however, was the thick woods that bordered on my paper route and the Connecticut and Hockanum rivers.

In 5th grade, I met another future close friend, Billy White, who was with me at the Borden's apartment during the loaded rifle incident. We played softball, sandlot football, and rode our bikes at 50 mph downhill, all without helmets or protective gear.

Once in a while, some friends and I "borrowed" some Coke bottles from the trucks that were parked and left unattended out in back of the Coca Cola bottling company on Main Street heading toward the south end. We didn't consider this stealing, since, after all, the bottles were left practically out in the open and not fenced in or protected or anything (stupid early-teenage rationalization).

My friends and I also were attracted to the large oil tanks that lined Riverside Drive on the banks of the Connecticut River. We liked to skim rocks, but instead of

The Coca Cola Bottling Company on south Main Street.

bouncing them off the water, we bounced them off two or three of these large tanks, which were probably 30 or 40 feet in diameter and approximately the same height. They contained a lot of oil brought up the river from all over the world. I should mention that when we were charged by the police for trying to blow up the town of East Hartford, our parents didn't think it was funny. We were lucky—they told us that a single spark from one of those rocks could have done it. We were released to our parents after promising never ever to set foot near the area again.

The site of our potentially disastrous rock-throwing incident. Back in the fifties, the river was home to many large oil tanks. This is now the location of Goodwin College.

Back at St. Mary's, I met Bonnie. We agreed to meet at the Saturday matinee show at the Eastwood Theater in the center of East Hartford. This was the method for going on a "date" in '59. You asked a girl to meet you at the Saturday matinee at the Eastwood Theater, "Dutch treat." That was my first date. I think we only met there a couple times. I liked her, but I had no confidence in myself at the time. I was immature, even for my age. In any event, I think the movie was Bill Haley and the Comets' "Rock Around the Clock." Rock 'n' roll was really exploding.

The misguided sisters at St. Mary's, however, hired a dance instructor to teach us how to "dance"—starting with the fox trot! Then they would march up and down the gym dance floor with a yardstick to make sure the Holy Ghost could fit between our bodies. *No touching!* was the rule. Some of the older guys would spit polish their shoes and claim they worked as mirrors to (supposedly) peek up their partner's dresses. The sisters, however, didn't take any chances and made everyone dance in their socks. No mirrors there!

Speaking of rock 'n' roll, Bo Diddley brought his band to the State Theater in Hartford. My folks were adamant that I could not attend. Friends of mine went and swore it was one of the best performances they'd seen. I was bummed.

Looking south toward Colt Street and the Aircraft Federal Credit Union (now Eagle Federal Credit Union), the Willow Inn, formerly Russell's Bar and Grill, is representative of the many south-end bars in the fifties.

Some people reading this might think we were a bunch of hooligans. But we were just kids from good families who were understandably a little rebellious toward the latter years of the narrow Catholic school experience. I mean, we really did like most of the sisters, and we knew that they had committed their lives to God and to helping us get an education—whether we wanted one or not.

Something changed, however, in our last year. I can't recall ever seeing either of the two sisters who taught our senior class smile. We were in 9th grade, which was as far as you could go at St. Mary's. And it seemed that a few of us were singled out for extra harassment. Maybe we warranted it, I really don't know. Looking back after all these years, we probably did. We were not exactly angels; however, we weren't devils, either.

One late spring day, we, as seniors, were supposed to have a "senior day off." However, it was decided instead—by the church Powers That Be—that due to the necessity of quickly getting the Sunday offering envelopes to the parishioners, we seniors needed to deliver these envelopes to selected sections of the parish.

In teams of three, we were directed to distribute the boxes that contained a year's worth of Sunday offering envelopes. We were less than excited—we figured that, at best, instead of a full day off, we would now only get maybe a quarter of the day off because of these envelopes and the distance to our assigned neighborhood. They foolishly put my two partners in crime, Frankie and Jimmy, with me.

So we three started walking. In addition to having a large territory, we had to walk to the Central Park area on the periphery of the parish boundaries. Along the way, a car with some nerdy-looking guys, who claimed they actually had been given the day off, stopped to ask for directions. We gave them directions—to Canada.

At the park, we sat on the side of a hill to rest for about 10 minutes. We looked at one another and didn't say a word. It was a true mind-to-mind psychic moment. We silently nodded to one another and started to dig with our hands into the side of the hill. We buried the boxes of envelopes and covered them up with grass and leaves. We vowed that this was to be a lifetime secret. Then we went off in different directions to enjoy our promised day off. We figured if the boxes were ever discovered, we would have long since graduated from St. Mary's and gone on to public high school.

The following Tuesday, I began to feel something amiss in the classroom. Sisters were whispering and moving hurriedly in and out of the classroom. Suddenly, the door flew open, and Frankie was called out to the hallway by Father O'Connor. Next was Jimmy Maloney and then me. It seemed like a scene from the Spanish Inquisition. Apparently, through what we all agreed was an act of Divine Providence, for the first time in history, a small tornado hit the very side of the hill where we had buried the envelopes. It led down to Central Park, which bordered the holiest of all the parish neighborhoods.

As a result of this freak tornado, thousands of holy pictures and envelopes were scattered throughout the area, landing in yards, gardens, rooftops, etc., of the devout and nondevout alike. Our parents were brought in and were (naturally) mortified when told that our names would be read at Sunday Mass like heretics in the Middle Ages.

I thought the saving grace of that year would be the class play, "Don't Take My Penney," which we practiced and rehearsed for a whole year and which had always been a major fundraiser for the graduation class trip to Coney Island. The play and the Coney Island trip had been a longstanding St. Mary's tradition. Fortunately

Central Park, site of the infamous "buried envelopes" caper.

for us, Jimmy and I were co-stars in the school play. As a result, we and our parents were given some leniency. We had to pay for the envelopes and do some work at the convent on weekends, but our names would not be read off at Sunday Mass. Whew!

Our worst punishment came from our folks, and we deserved it and probably more. This was an immature act. How could we ever have expected the cards would not be missed?

The absolute worst part of senior year came when our beloved pastor and school principal, Father Drennan, died. Everyone loved Father Drennan—he was a grandfatherly type who truly loved us like his own. The sisters had a hard time with him because he was so lenient. The following day, we were marched in formation across the street to St. Mary's Church to discuss the class trip —the one that had Coney Island as its long-anticipated destination and that was to be paid for in full with proceeds from the play.

Without skipping a beat, the sisters began by having us remember how much Father Drennan meant to us all and how much he loved us. Then they let us have it: They thought we should help build a monument to Father Drennan and use the money earmarked for our trip to Coney Island! I had wanted to go to Coney Island

and ride the Parachute Jump since 1st grade, and I couldn't believe what I was hearing! I thought, *Why can't they just hold one of their many—many!—special collections to pay for it?*

They went on to explain that they believed in the democratic system, and while they knew that everyone agreed with them, they would still have a vote. So they asked all fifty of us to close our eyes. Since they knew everyone would agree with their proposal, only those who didn't agree should raise their hands. Next they said, "Keep your hands up," and at the same time they ordered everyone to open their eyes.

There we sat, Frankie, Jimmy, and me, three out of fifty, with only our hands raised and all eyes focused accusingly on us. I knew that three-quarters of the class wanted to go to Coney Island but didn't have the courage to raise their hands.

We ended up going to Ocean Beach Park (New London, Connecticut) that year. It wasn't bad, but it wasn't Coney Island. Most of us never got to Coney Island. For a few spiteful moments, we two considered resigning from the play. But in the end, we *did* love Father Drennan, and also we couldn't let our classmates of the last nine years down. They were an extended family, akin to our brothers and sisters.

Next big item in the year was the prom. Girls were not allowed to wear strapless gowns, although some of them were 15 going on 21 in mind and body. To our surprise, a few of the more healthily endowed girls came to the convent for the review (inspection) wearing strapless gowns and received frowns from the nuns and envious stares from everyone else.

After pulling up enough courage from somewhere, I asked Geraldine to go with me. She gently and kindly declined, as she had already agreed to go with someone older from the high school. When I told Maloney, he said, "Hey, Norton (one of my nicknames), you only asked the prettiest girl in the class and maybe the town!" I didn't really consider that fact at the time. She was the Annette Funicello of St. Mary's and a sweet girl.

What did I know? I asked Carol, who was gracious and sweet. Her mother drove and afterward took us and Maloney and his date to the Marco Polo Restaurant after the dance. I realized there that I had forgotten my wallet, but I was too dense to even be embarrassed. I lucked out, though, as Jimmy had extra money. Like me, many of my St Mary's buddies were so awkward, but we had so many laughs!

During this period, catechism classes began for the kids who went to public school, and they were held at

St. Mary's. Afterward, they had a record hop in our gigantic gymnasium. This was obviously the real "hook" to get public school kids to come over and get indoctrinated. For us, even though it wasn't mandatory to attend, it was a way to meet and dance with the girls. Also, it was a sanctioned, legitimate way to get to stay out late on a school night.

The problem as I saw it was that the public school guys seemed 5 or 6 years older. They weren't really, but the girls seemed to find them more interesting than the immature guys they had known since kindergarten.

"Smoke Gets in Your Eyes," a song by the Platters, seemed to start every CYO dance, followed by Bobby Day's "Over and Over and Over Again." I loved the music, but even with the "dancing lessons" and all, my buddies and I had no innate rhythm or moves, so we watched the older public school guys steal our St. Mary's girls.

For us, the highlight of the weekly catechism class was having an Awful-Awful (a thick, thick milkshake introduced by Friendly's Ice Cream in New England in the late fifties) at the newly opened Friendly's on Main Street. The other highlight of the night out was when the bus dropped me off in front of the YWCA near Church Corners on the way to CCD, where I was often greeted by one of my sister's younger classmates, Judy, a blond cutie. Unfortunately, it wasn't cool to let a girl know you liked her!

>····<

After my paper route, we would play some of the toughest sandlot football games you could imagine. Until I began high school, I was about the same size as most all the guys. In high school, I got left behind and grew more slowly and stayed relatively short at 5'7". I was strong for my size and still am today, but I watched many of my buddies pass me in height.

When we weren't playing ball, we were in the woods by the river with our bows and arrows and our BB guns. We brought home squirrels, rabbits, muskrats, which we trapped, and pheasant. My mother, God bless her, would occasionally boil the unfortunate creature after I skinned it and feed it to my beagle, Kymo (a Gaelic name).

Kymo was my hunting partner. I once tied a long twine around our arrows and blindly fired into the sky above the river and struck a duck that took flight with hundreds of its species. That was one thing I couldn't bring myself to do—pluck feathers.

I had something of an epiphany one day after shooting a squirrel out of a tree (not an easy feat with a BB gun). The thought occurred to me: *Why did I do that?!* I never stopped exploring the woods, but that day, I made a private vow to never hurt another animal in my life, and I never did.

≻···≺

With Doug Sweet, my new next-door neighbor on Colt Street, we were "patrolling" a section of woods along

Ricky Dickman (right); and the author in "A White Sport Coat and a Pink Carnation," all dressed up for a prom [song by Marty Robbins, 1957].

Whatever Happened to the Pecords? 47

the Connecticut River not far from where it and the Hockanum River intersect. Suddenly, we saw what seemed to be an early Christmas present for us both. In the middle of nowhere, we found a wooden sailboat! You normally wouldn't see a sailboat out on the river. The current often seemed as fast as a motor boat. We assumed someone abandoned it, so we decided to try it out.

The fact that we had no boating, let alone sailing, experience never even entered our young minds. We put it into the water. In a few minutes, we figured out how to hoist the sail. Then, almost immediately, like another act of Divine Providence, the sky and air changed, and a gust whipped us out to the center of the river. Before we could comprehend our dilemma, another gust of wind, followed by a crack of thunder and a bolt of lightning, drove us back to the shore and into a tall dock.

These docks were built tall enough to accommodate the changing depth of the river and the huge barges that often moored there. That maneuver knocked the mast down, and back toward the middle of the river we went. Within minutes, we realized that we had no control, and heading out to the ocean at Old Saybrook was not completely out of the question.

Then we noticed a 40-foot cabin cruiser heading toward us, and we both took off our tee shirts and started waving frantically. The boat saw us and steered our way. They threw us a rope, and we asked to be towed to the spot where we originally found the sailboat.

The drama continued when the captain of an oil barge moored nearby stood on the deck and ordered the cabin cruiser to hold us while he called the police. The captain, holding a megaphone, shouted that he witnessed us stealing the boat! The cabin cruiser continued to tow us back and either didn't hear the barge captain or chose not to heed his "orders."

Back on shore, we secured the battered boat the best we could. That's when Doug found a hand-written note in the sand that must have blown off the boat. It read something along the lines of "This boat is private property. Do not touch." Holy cow, we thought, and began running.

As I have said so often, no one knew the woods and river like we did. We even had secret, hidden underground forts stocked with candles, Army C-rations, and more.

I never heard anything more about the boat. We both hoped that the damage wasn't too great. Again, who would leave a sailboat on the edge of the forest on the bank of a river with such a fast current? And you, reader, might be thinking, "And who would be so stupid as to take it out on that river?" All I can say is that this story is not attempting to make sense out of anything. It's just the way things were in our teenage small-town and blissfully ignorant "Stand by Me" fifties world.

≻····≺

Our entertainment was mostly furnished by ourselves and each other along with our gigantic imaginations. For some, life could get a little boring, but not for my buddies and me. If we didn't have something to do, we invented it. We pulled some really wild, stupid pranks. That's all I plan to say about that because I am not an expert in the statute of limitations laws, although I assume they have long since run out. But that's the way it was in East Hartford, Connecticut.

≻····≺

The other landmarks were mostly the neighborhood bars. Russell's was my father's favorite, and it was later sold to a famous East Hartford ex-policeman and neighbor of ours, Frank Benettieri. (Sadly, Frank passed away in 2011.) Another was Monti's, which was later owned by my friend Frankie Grandi's parents. You will recall Frankie from the St. Mary's Flat Top Boogie/Chicago haircut story.

Then there was the Cow Shed, which became Big Jim's and finally Gila's, owned by—guess who? Yep, Frank

Grandi owned it years later. The Yankee Grill became a little more famous when my friend Brian's older brother, Brett Hope, bought it. That's the south end.

My paper route had almost doubled, thanks to my hard work and budding salesmanship. However, the state decided to correct some traffic congestion and build what was to become Route 2. This cut through my end of town, and as quickly as my customer base had grown, it was diminished by a third from something called "eminent domain."

"There he is!" I heard one of the men shouting. I felt what I now know is a rush of adrenaline flash through my body. My daydreaming came to a sudden halt. I had to get to the Hockanum and the swing rope. I didn't compete in track, but this felt like the 100-yard dash—except that my pursuers were coming toward me at an angle. I couldn't believe how fast they were, considering their advanced age. But I knew they couldn't catch me, and I believed they had no idea of what I was going to do when I got to the muddy Hockanum River. I believe they thought I was trapped. It certainly looked that way.

≻...≺

I would always start my Friday night collections on Colt Street. About three-fourths of the way down the street, it became a dirt road. After Route 2 was completed, the street was cut in half. To get to the bottom (western) portion, you would have to walk under Route 2 via an underpass.

At the beginning of this dirt road extension was Banks' Hill, which was named after a family called Banks. I felt sad about the Banks family. The Banks boys were afflicted by what I was told was the result of their parents being first cousins. Sometimes the "boys" (although in their 30s or 40s) came out in diapers to pay me. Their older sister seemed to be in better shape and worked in Hartford. But I always got paid.

Banks' Hill was close to the Banks's home and provided some of the best sledding for our American Flyers you could find anywhere in the south end.

>···<

At the end of the Colt Street extension, and at the very edge of the Connecticut River, my last customer's house was owned by a family named Pecord. Initially, the household consisted of an elderly couple who looked like someone's grandparents; they were very nice people who always paid on time.

At some point, more people moved in. I believe they were the Pecord's daughter, her husband, and their two young children. I can't tell you why, but I immediately felt something was amiss with the husband. I did not like the guy. Why, I don't know, but I think that sometimes kids are intuitive. I continued to deliver my papers.

A bunch of "girlie" magazines accumulated on the bank of a hill next to the Pecord's house. I had no idea where they were coming from, but it seemed like someone was dumping a lot of risqué magazines down this embankment. Of course, at the ripe old age of 14 and 15, I couldn't stop myself from peeking through them when no one was around. However, that Friday night in fall 1959 would change my young life forever.

I knocked on the Pecord's door as usual. Nothing. I knocked a second time and got no answer. I peered in through the window in the door and noticed that the kitchen table was fully set with plates, etc. I also noticed that there seemed to be food on the plates. Still no answer. I left.

Saturday morning was also a collection day for me. I went back to 120 Colt Street. I knocked, and again no one came. This time I turned the door knob ever so slightly. It opened, and I felt compelled to ease my way in, calling out tentatively as I did, "Hello?...*Times*?...Collecting...?" But there wasn't an answer or any sound.

I immediately realized that the Pecord family was not there and had left quickly. There appeared to be spaghetti in a large pot still sitting on the stove. I got really nervous and practically ran out of the house.

I decided to go and get two of my buddies, Ricky and Dougie, to come with me. We made a solemn oath never to tell anyone about the event; however, both of them have passed on, and I feel it's time.

Upon our arrival early that same Saturday afternoon, we went through the house room by room. Everything seemed to be just left and in a little disarray, as if they had had to literally run out of the house. We left and promised each other we would not tell a soul.

On Monday evening, I was back delivering the *Hartford Times*, so I decided to try once more. I knocked, and no one came. The plates and everything seemed untouched, exactly as on the previous days. Again, I decided to open the door and go in. I again went from room to room calling out, but the house was hollow—empty.

It was in one of the bedrooms facing the river that I noticed a dresser drawer pulled open, displaying some lady's jewelry. I didn't know if they were real diamonds and real gold—or who might have been in the house since my buddies and I went through it on Saturday afternoon. Who found this stuff, and why hadn't it been taken when the Pecords left? I turned and saw the light sliding across the room from the setting sun shimmering across the Connecticut River.

Immediately, I noticed that the wallpaper had been torn in places, as if someone were trying to find something. I followed what looked like a trail of rips and slits in the wall, which to my amazement led to a metal 2' X 3' door, which was slightly opened. The crude metal

From the East Hartford side, looking across the Connecticut River at the blue onion dome of the Colt Firearms Factory, exactly as I noticed it while making my escape.

The of the original Colt Armory was built in 1855 and was a central part of Samuel Colt's firearms-making empire. Based in the district of Hartford known as Coltsville, the armory was later joined by additional buildings, including housing for workers. The Colt mansion, Armsmear, was built on a nearby hill, overlooking the factory complex. In 1864, three years after Colt's death, the original armory was destroyed by fire. It was then rebuilt by Colt's widow, Elizabeth Colt, using designs by the company's general manager, General William B. Franklin. The new building was designed to be fireproof and was larger than its predecessor. It was also more decorative, with a design based on the styles of the Italian Renaisssance.

door had wallpaper glued on the outside that matched the rest of the room. I peered into what looked like a homemade wall safe, now empty. I felt panicked again and ran out of the house.

The next evening I rushed to deliver all my papers, excluding the Pecords'. I returned home and called my buddies, who agreed to meet me in the woods in back of my home. I decided to take my Red Ryder BB gun and also avoid the street, so we took a famliar path through the thick woods along the Willow Brook. Just before the brook took a right turn to head toward the Hockanum River, we veered to the left and proceeded up the embankment that would put us in front of the Pecords' house.

As I was brushing away vines and thorn bushes in the dense vegetation, a glint of light shone on a metal object. In a split second, from the corner of my eye, I saw a car covered with branches on my far left. *What the heck?* I thought. The setting sun shone on two men nearby, one of whom was smoking a cigarette.

This whole scene unfolded in a matter of seconds. After I whispered urgently to my friends to stay back, without skipping a beat, instead of walking across the small dirt cul-de-sac, I quickly turned right, heading away from the Pecord's house toward a 6-foot-wide trail that led to the Hockanam River, pretending that I had not seen anything.

I heard the car doors open and slam shut, but I didn't look back. Instead, I slung my BB gun over my shoulder and started to walk in quick time. I thought I felt someone running behind me, but I wouldn't look back and acknowledge my worst fears. I began to run, and then I heard one of the men yell, "Hey, kid, stop!"

I remember thinking, *Yeah, right*. A thought flashed through my mind that maybe these men were cops. However, they didn't yell, "Stop! Police!" I probably wouldn't have stopped anyhow, because I was a very skeptical and spooked kid. I would have needed proof, and I wasn't about to stop and take a chance.

They never identified themselves. I figured that whoever they were, they were maybe looking for the missing contents of that safe. I didn't take anything—but would they have believed me? I didn't think so. I was running at full speed, but they were close, and I could hear heavy breathing. Luckily for me, I had stamina going for me, because of all the stupid, crazy things I did do, I never got hooked on cigarettes like a lot of my young friends already had.

I quickly turned left into the thick forest that lined the river bank; again, I knew exactly where I was and where

I was going. I didn't plan on getting caught, like Doug and I were in the embarrassing peashooter incident.

We were still running at what seemed like top speed. I could see the Charter Oak Bridge in the distance, and I was surprised and a little worried that they (whoever they were) had kept up.

A few months earlier, a friend had helped us rig a huge long rope swing that allowed us to swing from one side of the Hockanum clear across to the other side, not far from where it entered the Connecticut River. Right now I was praying that the rope was where it was supposed to be—on the south side of the Hockanum—the side I was on.

I dove into a gully and began crawling on my belly. There was a huge oak tree on my left, a tiny hint of autumn color on its leaves, so I crawled behind it unseen, or so I hoped. The two men went flying past me, and I began to feel relieved. Unfortunately, fear took hold again, and I was aware of feeling mentally stuck there—my body was pretty much frozen even though it was a warm early fall evening. I was also amazed at how fast a couple of older guys could run. Thank goodness—they were gone, and I sat and caught my breath.

Who were they? Why were they chasing me? Did it have something to do with the family that had gone missing a couple evenings before? Did they know my friends and I had gone into the house? All these questions and more flooded my brain. For one of the first times in my young life, I was scared, really scared. The sun was beginning to set, and looking into the trees, I could see its rays flickering across the river.

As I cowered behind the tree, I believed my life was in danger. As students at St. Mary's, we did a lot of praying, so I began to pray to Our Lord for my two friends and me, even though I was pretty sure at least they got away unharmed, thanks to my quick reflexes.

Suddenly I heard branches cracking and other indistinguishable noises north of me. *Uh-oh*, I thought, *they're still looking*.

I slowly peeked around the tree. I could see the guy with the hat moving through a patch of five- to six-foot reeds. His partner was not with him, so I assumed they had split up. I heard more movement to the right and caught a glimpse of the other man's head. My problem was that they were blocking my passage northward to safety. I considered heading back to toward the Pecord's house, but what if there were a third person guarding the car who might see me if I returned?

I figured I had to get across the Hockanum River, which emptied into the Connecticut River about 500 yards from where I was hiding. My friends and I knew the woods and the river better than anyone. At the Hockanum, we had a secret raft to carry us across; however, it was heavily secured and would take time to free it. That left another swing rope we kept on a hook imbedded into one of the many large trees that hung gracefully out over the Hockanum. I decided on the rope.

Without another thought, I sprang forward to a cluster of trees and bushes, landing on my knee. Unluckily, my knee struck a rock, which tore open my jeans, and blood spurted out. I wanted to yell out in pain, but I knew I mustn't. For someone who was as cocky and confident about the forest as I was, the situation was disheartening, particularly with a wound on my knee and the possibility of leaving a blood trail. I was suddenly thankful they didn't have a dog with them. I pulled my body into the thicket and hid as best I could, hoping that whoever they were, they would eventually give up. (I still have a close to one inch scar on my knee even after 50+ years of shrinkage. Since I felt I couldn't tell anyone, it never got properly sutured.)

My mind started to drift a little due to mental exhaustion, and I began remembering earlier years when I lived about 400 yards east of my current location at United

Homes. It was there that I got my first introduction to these brooks and rivers and the thick forest. The United Homes Housing project actually abutted the woods. The project housed mostly the employees of Pratt & Whitney, such as my father. During the war there were a lot of military units stationed nearby, so we had plenty of leftover foxholes to explore and use to build our imaginations.

For a while everything seemed surrealistically quiet. Memories of my young life glided thru my mind at a rapid rate. I thought of my family, my mom and dad and my younger sister Kathleen, and how worried they would be if I didn't show up in time for dinner. I thought of my home on Colt Street and East Hartford. It was all I knew then, except for our family's annual vacation in August to Rockaway Beach in Queens, New York, when Pratt & Whitney shut down for two weeks.

I heard a loud whistle coming from a little way off toward the northeast. It definitely sounded human, so I shinnied up a young oak tree to get a look. I noticed one of the men waving to his partner, who began running toward him. Please don't let it be Ricky or Dougie. It wasn't. They began pulling and tugging at something. I think they had discovered one of our many underground forts (courtesy of the U.S. Army).

Our forts were well hidden and usually stocked with Army C-rations, lanterns, and often cigarettes. I never smoked much, but a lot of my friends did. I tried it once in a while to act cool and tough, but basically hated it. Didn't realize at the time, but my smoking abstinence provided me with some extra stamina.

They must have thought I was hiding inside one of the tunnels. Great diversion from me! So I scrambled toward the river to get away from the thick vegetation and pricker bushes, as I called them. Even with my jeans and long-sleeved shirt, my arms and legs were cut to ribbons, and I was bleeding everywhere. For some reason, I forgot about my knee and started running along the river, which was lined by trees. However, they were not thickly placed, and the growth around them had been killed by many of the river's overflows. The sun's reflection on the water was almost blinding.

This enabled me to make some good time moving toward the river. I must have gained another hundred yards toward my destination, the Hockanum River. In the distance, I could even see the underbelly of the huge Charter Oak Bridge, which marked the Hockanum's entrance into the Connecticut River. It's very difficult to explain the effects of my fatigue, both mentally and physically—unless you have been in a dangerous situation, one possibly involving life and death, it is hard to comprehend. This was combined with the fact that I was being hunted by men who I didn't know.

While in the Pecord house, we did find a crude tin home safe, the door covered by wallpaper, swinging open in a wall, empty! This was couple of days after I first saw that the Pecords's house had been pretty much abandoned. Somebody must have taken something. I wondered if it were possibly that money was moved and buried out back temporarily. It became apparent to me as I ran for my life that someone thought it might have been us. Great.

Mickey's Oceanic Grill drive-in on Pitkin Street; established in 1953, it was known for its fresh seafood. The dike that ran behind Mickey's was constructed by the Army Corps of Engineers after the 1938 hurricane to protect the town from the rivers.

The sound of twigs and branches snapping close by had me perspiring profusely. I needed something to drink. I felt like I was going to pass out....

I could see the rope about 200 feet away. I found to my relief that I was getting a second wind. I got to the rope, unhooked it, and made a running leap with it across the river. I landed splat! in the mud on the river's north side.

I unslung my Red Ryder BB gun while scrambling up the bank. I saw that one of them seemed to be looking for something, while the other guy just kept staring. Neither wore a patrolman's uniform. Then I noticed his partner coming with a large broken tree branch. What the heck? I thought again. He was actually going to try and grab the rope left dangling over the center of the river!

In my young brain, it was a life-or-death moment. So I started firing near them to divert their attention and to give myself some time to escape. I am sure after a few rounds, they realize I didn't have a .22, but it startled them, and one guy started waving his hand like when you experience pain. It must have been an unintentional ricochet shot. I think I hit his finger.

The sun, rapidly sinking behind me, sparkled on something metallic. I thought, *Gun*. I don't know for sure if it

The Hockanum River near its entrance into the Connecticut River. The rope is gone, but you can easily envision one hanging from one of the trees.

Example of the dense forest about 100 feet from the river.

was, but I didn't wait to find out. I headed north along the river, and—thank God!—I heard no shots.

At last, I made my way huffing and puffing north along the Connecticut River and ended up near Pitkin Street. Pitkin Street was home to another great drive-in restaurant, Mickey's Oceanic Grill Drive-In. Mickey's was known for their fish and clams.

There, in back of Mickey's, I buried my rifle under some leaves and branches, and then continued walking casually along the swamp side of the dike that had been erected there by the Army Corps of Engineers after the Great Hurricane of 1938.

I waited until it was completely dark before I made my way back home using Main Street. Of course, I stayed close to some of the large homes and away from the street and lights as much as possible. I arrived home exhausted and got a scolding for missing dinner.

After school the next afternoon, I connected with my buddies Ricky and Doug. First and foremost, they were safe! Second, unbeknownst to me, they never left! Instead, they followed the chase as closely as possible while remaining invisible to my pursuers and dreading the worst. When through the dense trees and vines they blurrily saw me swinging on our rope across to the north side of the Hockanum, they knew it was okay to go home. They were just as glad to see that I was all right as I was to see that they were all right.

Probably because of my age, I took their actions for granted; however, over the years, I came to realize the chance they took, which gave even more meaning to their friendship and loyalty. To this very day, I still hear Benney King's lyrics when I think of them and our adventure.

> *Stand by me,*
> *Won't you stand by me....*

Wordlessly, we clapped each other on the back and entered the woods that abutted my back yard on Colt Street. We made our way along the Willow Brook, which twisted and turned to join the Hockanum near its mouth on the Connecticut just before the Charter Oak Bridge. Doug and I had our BB guns. That day, I let Ricky use mine, as this time I had brought my wooden bow with about 20 arrows. (I am not bragging, but I was like the Robin Hood of East Hartford, having won several bow and arrow contests in the surrounding area.) What we planned to do with these armaments, I had no clue. It just made us feel safer, I guess.

When we got to the vicinity of the Pecord's house, we once again crawled quietly through the thick brush.

There they were! Although we weren't a hundred percent sure, they looked like the two guys who chased me except no hat plus different clothes. This time they were digging feverishly. One guy had a shovel on the house side of the stone wall that ran to the river, which had been part of the original ferry stop. The other guy was digging or uncovering something on the other side of the wall facing the woods.

It was difficult to see exactly what was going on without putting ourselves in harm's way. I strung my bow and placed an arrow on the string, and Doug and Ricky cocked their BB guns; then we just rested there trying to see through the thick vines. Abruptly, one of the guys looked in our direction. Maybe he heard the rifles being cocked. We didn't know, but we weren't about to stick around and find out.

We slid on our backsides down the hill and sprinted like three jackrabbits back to the Willow Brook and the woods. We made it home in about 20 minutes, nervous and proud of our courage (some would say recklessness) to even attempt to go back after what had happened the evening before. That was the last time I looked at the house at 120 Colt Street for many years.

≻⋯≺

The following Saturday, I was delivering papers as usual. I decided that since it was still daylight, I would try and peek toward the end of the dirt road where the Pecord house was. As I was about to try to get a closer look, a policeman pulled up and asked what I was doing there.

It was all I could do to not choke and stammer. Instead, I managed to say nonchalantly, "Oh, just delivering the *Hartford Times*." Then I asked what was going on down the street, motioning to the Pecord's house. The officer studied me for a few seconds and then said, "Stay away from that place, kid. Something is going on there. Just keep away." Which I studiously did for a long, long time.

>···<

I always felt that something horrible happened that evening back in 1959. Why didn't I (we) immediately call the police? We respected them, but we felt that maybe someone would try to pin something on us. It was a different time, more innocent—hard to understand if you didn't grow up in the fifties. Remember, no cell phones, no 911. Just "Dial 0 for Operator" and plenty of rampant imagination.

Later in life, any time I was in the area, I was drawn to the house, and I'd drive by to look. Just to look—and to wonder what happened to that nice old couple, mostly, but also to their children and grandchildren. I noticed that someone remodeled it at some point, and it looked like United Aircraft did some work in back.

I asked friends about it. The late Frank Benettieri, a police officer before he bought the Willow Inn, said that he would check with some of his friends on the force, but nothing surfaced. I asked my childhood friend, John Choquette, who became assistant mayor, to see if he could get me some time at the police station to view records. I called there myself but was informed that the records are only kept for 10 years. I couldn't ascertain whether I would be able to find anything on microfilm.

So after all these years, I don't know what ever happened to the Pecords. There might be a simple answer, but the questions remain. Were they spirited away by criminals or aliens? Did someone, maybe one of the older couple, get sick and die suddenly? Were they placed into a witness protection program? Who chased me and why? What about that homemade wall safe? And what about the digging around by the outside wall? What was that all about? In any event, we kept our oath and didn't tell a soul that we were in that house by the river in 1959.

> *...The night has come,*
> *And no, no, I won't be afraid*
> *Just as long as you stand*
> *Stand by me.*

Whatever Happened to the Pecords?

≻...≺

I told Sharon, my wife of 40-plus years, that if any of my kids did even half the stuff I did, I'd be fuming. But that was me and that was the fifties, and things were different. I loved the era. I'm pleased to say that I had the opportunity to apologize to the good sisters for all my youthful antics at a St. Mary's 9th-grade class reunion in the late 1970s. It was organized by Geoff Callahan, a classmate who became the owner of Callahan Funeral.

You might be thinking that a number of high school classes have never had a reunion, and yet this guy is talking about a 9th-grade reunion. You're right, it is out of the ordinary—maybe even a little bizarre. But by now you must also be thinking that my whole fifties experience was bizarre, and you are probably right. St. Mary's was more like an extended family—after all, we all grew up together. Many kids were much like brothers or sisters. All I can offer is this: If it hadn't been so crazy and bizarre, I wouldn't have had much to write about.

I still get together with Bill White, who lives in Manchester, Connecticut, with his wife Arlene and children and grandchildren, and I occasionally see Jim Maloney who resides in Dallas, Texas. We still talk about the "good old days," and I make sure I toast my two departed

"Stand By Me" buddies, Ricky Dickman and Doug Sweet. God bless!

Frankie Grandi sold Gilas, formerly the Cow Shed (one of the numerous bars in the south end) and moved to Florida. It appears that Goodwin College is buying up a lot of the landmarks in the south end including Gilas, and I heard they purchased 120 Colt Street and possibly will tear it down. Nothing stays forever!

I always had unique experiences. When you get a chance, you can go to my Key Publishing Company website—*www.KeyPublishingCompany.com*—and click on the Articles page and read about what I call my "Forrest Gump" trip to Woodstock in 1969!

Appendix

Our Fifties "Secret" Family Vacations

When Pratt & Whitney shut down, as it did every August for the first two weeks, our family boarded a train in Hartford, which brought us to Grand Central Station in New York City. Occasionally, we would take the subway to Washington Heights, Upper Manhattan, and meet up with our cousins the Hughes family. Often we would all leave together via subway to Queens and our vacation destination, Rockaway Beach.

One of the many nervous flashbacks that I experienced during my escape was of Rockaway Beach. At the time, the flashback took only seconds, but when putting it down on paper, I felt it might be a distraction from the story.

However, like other flashbacks, the experience was part of my life and the era. I call it *secret* because no one that I knew had any firsthand knowledge of it other than what I would describe to them on our return. I say no one in East Hartford knew of it, *except* for one family that possibly hailed from that town.

Rockaway Beach Playland—1950s.

Rockaway Beach Boardwalk, once known as the Irish Riviera, Queens, New York.

There was a family named Hopkins, whose aunt my mother knew and who had a son named Bernard and a daughter whose name was Rose. I never confirmed that they were the family who lived in town. If they were, they must have some of same great memories.

Rockaway had the best surf and one of the longest fifties boardwalks on the East Coast. Many thought the Drifters' popular song of day, "Under the Boardwalk," was written about Atlantic City. It was not; it was written for the Rockaway boardwalk, which had a playland or amusement park with a rollercoaster that seemed to hang out over the ocean.

There weren't any hotels—only 4- and 5-storey rooming houses and some bungalows. Rockaway is where I tasted my first pizza and Italian ice. Almost every corner had and Irish pub with jigs and reels playing day and night. Thus it received its nickname "the Irish Riviera."

In addition to Irish music, rock and roll was making its debut and walking around the streets of Rockaway one could hear the Elegants sing "Twinkle, Twinkle, Little Star" and "Cathy's Clown" by the Everly Brothers. It was such a huge reprieve from the summer heat of the United Homes Housing Project; the sounds of seagulls, the clean smells emanating from the ocean's pristine salt water, the sounds of the carousel. I recall stopping in front of our Rockaway guesthouse, referred to as Brady's, to make sure that my shirt collar was turned up in the back—á la Elvis. *Thank your very muuach!*

Chuck Berry's "Johnny B. Goode" was blasting from one of the guest rooms. I loved the music. I loved Rockaway. And I really, really liked Kathy Goff, who regularly stayed with her family at Brady's guesthouse—but what do you know at 14 or 15? When I think of Rockaway Beach, playland, and boardwalk, I think of what my children must have thought of the first time we all went to Disneyland. The feeling—the exhilaration—must be experienced; describing it just doesn't do it justice.

If you have ever taken a Dale Carnegie Course on communications, you have learned how to remember things and events by association. For me, I believe the music enables me to remember and to recall events so long ago.

I started to learn to play the guitar. I never got very far, but the *music* changed me forever.

> *February made me shiver*
> *With every paper I delivered.*
> *Bad news on the on the door step*
> *I couldn't take one more step*
> *I can't remember if I cried*
> *When I read about his widowed bride*

> *But something touched me deep inside*
> *The day the music died.*

As you have read, the core of my tale took place on my *Hartford Times* paper route, 1959—"With every paper I delivered..."—what a coincidence! For me, "(Bye, Bye Miss) American Pie" by Don McLean is a prime example of my associating events with music.

One personal note: My friend and Merrill Lynch Financial Advisor Gary Venable was a classmate of Don McLean at Iona College in New York. I envision young Gary stepping out onto the Quad and witnessing a fellow student he barely knew sitting with a guitar and penning the words and notes for a song that would come to define our generation.

And speaking of loving the fifties hit songs, for those of you who remember (as I do), September 7, 2011, would have been Buddy Holly's 75th birthday! He died in February 1959 at age 22. He inspired and pioneered rock 'n' roll. Even the Beatles were inspired. Look at their names: "Buddy Holly and the Crickets" and "the Beatles"—coincidence—?!

Growing up fairly poor, I think I wanted to have something just for myself, a one-up on my friends. It made me feel a little superior having known this place called Rockaway for so many unforgettable summers.

I had heard rock 'n roll back in East Hartford, but for whatever reason hearing the early music and doo wop songs while vacationing in Rockaway—along with the unforgettable sounds of seagulls and surf, the clean smell of the greenish-gray saltwater, not to mention the rides, the roar of the Atom Smasher, and more—embedded them into my young teenage mind forever.

Thinking back, this magic place was the precursor to Disneyland and Disney World, only with waves. It also was a part of my Irish heritage. At Rockaway, my folks said they could mingle (as they would say it) with their "own kind," meaning that Rockaway attracted thousands of other Irish immigrants and their families. In a way, it allowed a poor kid to feel a little vicarious snobbishness for a couple of weeks and for a few months afterward while bragging to his buddies of all those wonderful experiences.

≻···≺

> As I was completing this book, a violent storm named Sandy struck the East Coast and ravaged Rockaway, the Jersey Shore, Staten Island, New York City and many of the beach towns in my state of Rhode Island. Needless to say, my prayers go out to everyone who was affected by this tragedy.
>
> —JPN

≻···≺

Closing Remarks

My name is Jim Naughton, and I first want to thank you, the reader, for your interest in my book(s). My first book, *Jump In and Start Swimming*, is now distributed all over the world. Please feel free to view it along with my Key Publishing Company website: *www.keypublishingcompany.com*.

I don't pretend to be a literary genius as I have repeatedly told my editor, Martha. I do believe I am a good storyteller, and most of my stories are true. I feel blessed to have had a lot of unique experiences over the years, and if I find somebody even casually interested, I will often and spontaneously start telling one of them. (Just ask my wife, Sharon.) In fact if you do happen to read my first book, which I refer to as a self-help and multi-informational with a documentary of my unique career. You will note that I "made a living" thru selling, and my sales presentations always consisted of stories. It was recently pointed out to me, that throughout history, many of the great teachers of the world employed stories to make their point

I have been queried regarding, why it took so long to get this story published—approximately 53 years—and the answer is twofold. First, my teenage buddies and I swore we would never tell anyone about the incident, because at the time we were convinced that something really awful happened in 1959, and we didn't want to be blamed. As they have both now passed on, I don't see any harm in sharing my experience of 53 years ago.

Even though we didn't do anything wrong, I sincerely hope that any statute of limitations has run out. Second, as our lives often dictate, we become engrossed in getting an education and then having a career, marriage, family, etc. So unless your career is one in the writing field, you find that you don't have a lot of time, and it takes a lot of time to write and publish.

I must admit that as a parent and a grandparent, my fond reminiscences about some of the outrageous and dangerous stunts of my past would not be appreciated (to put it mildly) by my children or wife. In fact, I initially considered writing the book in third person to hide my identity. It just wouldn't do. I am not trying to glorify any of my youth; I am just presenting exactly and honestly to the best of my recollection how things were.

In truth, my friends and I grew up reading Hank Ketchum's "Dennis the Menace" in comic books, then watched him on TV; years later, we realized that we (or at least some of us) had unknowingly, at the time, become little Dennises, sling shot hanging from the back pocket of our trousers and all. I am hoping you will agree with my premise that our Baby Boomer era was made more exciting by the Dennis the Menace types among us.

While I thoroughly enjoyed the movie "Stand by Me" and thought it was a great depiction of the late fifties, I also know that the story was fiction. My story is not only *non*fiction, but yours truly is the main character. I have often thought over the years, "If the world enjoyed 'Stand by Me' so much, maybe it would enjoy a true-life Stand-By-Me type of story."

Kudos to author Stephen King for his novella "The Body," which became the movie "Stand By Me," directed by Rob Reiner. And thank you, Benny King, for your memorable song. All of them inspired me to finally, after so many years, tell my story.

> *...The night has come*
> *And no I won't be afraid*
> *As long as you stand by me.*

Over the years, when passing through my home town of East Hartford, Connecticut, on my way back to Rhode Island, I would drive down the dirt road to the end of the Colt Street extension and just sit in my car and stare at the house, the river, and the woods and wonder if the whole episode was just crazy fifties teenage imagination. And I would remember the families who seemed to vanish into thin air.

I often told my wife I believed that I would probably find out what really happened to them if I ever got the story published. I am still hopeful for that! What I will never accept is any explanation of why I was chased and why I believed I was going to be harmed by at least the one of them who carried a gun. What were they doing with shovels in the backyard on the following day? Were they burying something or looking for something?

Thanks to Todd Andrews, of Goodwin College, I became aware of how my street (also the street location of the Pecords' house) got its name. It was named for Samuel Colt, owner of the Colt Firearms Company, who decided to build a ferry station there in East Hartford to allow his East Hartford machinists an alternative to paying a hefty toll when crossing the only bridge to and from Hartford. Ironically, the house at 120 Colt Street was also on property originally owned by Samuel Colt. It's still unclear, but it's just possible that the site may have been part of the ferry landing, as the house was located 50 feet from the river and close to the ferry. There is also the likelihood that Colt actually lived in the house. I have started to speculate that the wall safe that we located may have dated back to his time and of the possibility that later occupants were simply not aware of it. Somebody, however, was!

Another coincidence occurred when I first met Goodwin College's Todd Andrew via a phone conversation. He informed me that Goodwin had just purchased the house at 120 Colt Street and was planning to tear it down and build the college president's house on the land. When I told Todd about the book and my knowledge of the house back in 1959, he invited me come for a visit to Goodwin College and take a last look inside 120 Colt Street. To say it felt weird being inside the house is an understatement. Of course, it had changed over the years. My understanding is that it had been remodeled at least three times. However, the location of homemade wall safe was still embedded in my mind after all these years, and I was able to point to the site as part of the chimney structure jutting out in the second floor bedroom closest to the river, as I saw it back so long ago.

Later in the day, I drove to Founders Plaza, near the Connecticut River. As I began to take pictures for the book, I particularly wanted to make sure that I included a picture of the blue onion dome that graced the top the Colt Firearms factory on the Hartford side of the Connecticut River. To accomplish this, I parked my car at the foot of the Founders Bridge on the East Hartford side. The bridge has a park-like pedestrian walkway where I assumed that I could get a good shot of the dome. When I arrived at the bridge, I immediately noticed walkers and joggers heading south on a paved path along the river, so instead of taking the bridge stairs, I followed them.

After ten minutes of brisk walking, I notice a familiar site from over 50 years ago: There, in a clearing, was a sandy beach and a view of the Colt Firearms Factory and its blue onion dome over on the Hartford side of the river—the very scene that was deeply etched into my memory as I was being chased more fifty years ago.

I continued along the path, which cut through what was once dense forest and came upon the Hockanum River (Indian name for "hooked river," according to Goodwin College's historians, because of its early hooked path), flowing hurriedly under the many tall oak, maple, and cottonwood trees. My mind's eye remembered our swing rope. I was in awe. It was more than 50 years since I last stood here. I just kept staring when suddenly I was jolted out my daydream state. Standing behind me was a tall man dressed in what appeared to be a park ranger uniform, leaning against his vehicle.

He asked if I needed any help, and of course I asked who he was. He told me his name was Jim Egan and that he was a park ranger for a non-profit organization—River Front Recapture.

River Front Park ranger Jim Egan. Jim works for the private, nonprofit Riverfront Recapture. The park exists where my buddies and I once hunted, built rafts, and allowed our imaginations to blossom. For more information go to www.riverfront.org.

Modern-day view of Riverfront Park, created a few years back in the dense forest that bordered the river.

To my amazement, it began to sink in that my old stomping ground—the forest, Willow Brook, and the Hockanum and Connecticut rivers—were now part of a major park area. This wonderful place, which allowed my friends and me to let our imaginations run wild and to imagine ourselves as Davy Crockett, Huckleberry Finn, and Tom Sawyer, is now a beautiful park for everyone to enjoy. And it was constructed without actually disturbing the pristine ambience I remember as a kid!

Thanks to River Front Recapture and everyone who has contributed to this nonprofit organization, my grandchildren will be able to accompany me and actually come close to experiencing the kind of wonder I felt as I explored this area many years ago. Who knows? They may even bring *their* children and grandchildren here in the future. I love thinking that.

Whatever Happened to the Pecords?   85

I am convinced my story could only have taken place in the 1950s. Back then, we rode our bicycles down a hill at speeds exceeding 40 mph without helmets; we crashed our American Flyer sleds into one another, again, without helmets. We kids, boys of the fifties, were invincible—or so we thought. Fearless, we built forts and tree houses, fell out of trees, constructed rudimentary rafts out of logs, and considered them river-worthy; we were at the same time naïve; innocent. We took these traits with us into the sixties and into life.

I thought I was tough and in good physical shape until my first day of boot camp in January 1964. I wasn't afraid until after the first day. Naïve? No one except for a certain few knew what was coming—a place called Vietnam. Many thousands of the later-fifties generation went over to 'Nam, fearlessly. After all, we

View of Goodwin College from the west. The docks are the original docks that my friends and I fished from in the fifties. The college has refurbished them, thus allowing the replica of explorer Henry Hudson's tall ship the Half Moon to dock for visitors each summer. In the distance, one can see the famous Pratt & Whitney Aircraft jet engine manufacturer.

grew up thinking we were invincible; we played sandlot tackle football almost every night during the fall football season. We grew up shooting at one another with various toy weapons. No one ever really got hurt, right? We watched World War II army movies in which a young soldier lay wounded on the battlefield and all he ever asked for was…a cigarette?!

My first job upon returning home from a stint in Paris Island was an apprentice power linesman for Hartford Electric Light (HELCO). I climbed 40-foot-tall electric poles with a pair of hooks and a belt and earned the right to work on the secondary (120-volt) wires. Wasn't I scared climbing those poles? No. As I have said I (we) grew up during the fifties; we were invincible. (I should mention that now, when I change a light bulb in our kitchen ceiling utilizing a 4-ft (not 40-ft) stepladder, my wife, Sharon, is usually standing close, holding the ladder and me!)

Finally, I honestly believe that I recall so much about the era because of the music. I simply unknowingly employed the technique of association while rock 'n' roll was evolving. The oldies, as we now call them, were the newest rage. Dick Clark's "American Bandstand" was a show we all watched after school. It was where we really learned to dance…at least where some of us did. After Carl Perkins, we watched Elvis shaking his hips and lower torso on the Ed Sullivan Show. He and Jerry Lee Lewis were making million-dollar records. Dion DiMucci of Dion and the Belmonts was "stoop singing, *a cappella* style" in the Bronx:

> *Here's my story,*
> *It's sad but true,*
> *It's about a girl I once knew,*
> *She took my love then ran around*
> *With every single guy in town…*

Wikipedia and other sources state that Tommy Allsup lost a coin toss for a seat on the ill-fated plane heading to Moorhead, Minnesota, with Dion DiMucci opting out of the expensive flight. Years later, at a live 50s show, Dion gave a group of us his recollection, in which he himself won that coin toss but let his ticket be sold instead to Ritchie Valens ("La Bamba"), who joined Buddy Holly ("Peggy Sue") and Jiles Perry "J. P." Richardson, Jr.—the Big Bopper ("Chantilly Lace" ("Hello, Baby!")) for the plane ride to Moorhead. Minutes after takeoff, their plane crashed in a cornfield in a heavy snowstorm...no survivors. It's no wonder with the death of the pioneers of rock 'n' roll that this tragic event became known as "The Day the Music Died."

It was so devastating that it is still discussed in 2013. These early rock 'n' rollers included Chuck Berry and Little Richard, and they all inspired the Beatles, the Rolling Stones, and many others of their generation. Movies like Bill Haley and the Comets's "Rock Around the Clock" and James Dean's "Rebel Without a Cause" were defining pieces of our era. It was different in the cities versus the rural areas, but we Baby Boomers were all affected by the 1950s and vice versa.

I still recall events from the day when I hear a familiar "oldie." It was a special time; a fun time of imagination, a time of 8-inch oval-screen Emerson TVs with rabbit ears antennae and a "test pattern" at the end of the broadcasting day. No cell phones. In fact, many will remember the "party lines" and politely telling your neighbors you needed to use the phone for an emergency two-minute call. As previously mentioned, the fifties influenced and shaped the Baby Boomers, as we are called, in ways that I am still learning. It really was "Happy Days."

I should also mention that around the time of the vanishing of the two families, my buddies and I were fishing not far from that house when I hooked what I thought was a large carp—some grew to 40 pounds and more. It turned out to be a bloated body. This we *did* tell our folks, and they reported it to the police. Of course, the police never told us what or who it was. There was rumor that someone from Pecords' house fell out of a canoe. Of course, I have a hard time believing that someone would be on that fast-moving river in a canoe; however, yours truly went out—inexperienced!—in a sailboat. Was the body a piece of the puzzle? I don't know.

And yes, almost 53 years later, every now and then I *do* wonder to myself, *"Whatever happened to the Pecords??"**

Goodwin College Today

"The mission of Goodwin College is to educate a culturally diverse student population in an environment that builds bridges between education, commerce, and community. Our degree and certificate programs prepare students for professional careers while encouraging lifelong learning and promoting civic responsibility.

Goodwin College's main academic and administration building on the bank of the Connecticut River, East Hartford. The college (www.goodwin.edu) is expanding rapidly, working with the town and also Riverfront Recapture, as much of the campus is located on the Connecticut River. Note that the original site was home to General Oil Company.

Aerial view of the Goodwin College campus looking north along the Connecticut River. In the distance, you can see the Charter Oak Bridge— this marks the spot where the Hockanum River makes its entry into the Connecticut River and that was the approximate site of our rope tree swing. The city of Hartford lies just beyond to the northwest. A little more than midway to the bridge you can see the high wire tower.

"As a nurturing college community, we challenge students, administration, faculty and staff to realize their academic, professional and personal potential."

The college is happy to share the link to their webcam, so the reader can view the core area of the story.
http://webcam.goodwin.edu/view/index.shtml

***Please consider contributing your
tax-deductible dollars to
this wonderful organization.***

Riverfront Recapture is a unique private, non-profit organization dedicated to improving central Connecticut's quality of life and urban vitality through cultural events, entertainment, group sports, and recreation in a welcoming environment along the banks of the Connecticut River. It also supports ongoing efforts to protect and maintain the riverfront and make more of it accessible to the public.

It is the first and only organization in the region to offer this combination of programming, all designed to connect people to the river, get them back in touch with nature within an urban environment, and provide them with experiences they might not otherwise have.

Riverfront Recapture began in 1981 with the goal of transforming the banks of the Connecticut River from an area walled off by flood dikes and cut off by Interstate 91 into a vibrant, active riverfront of four parks connected by riverwalks and bridges. The Riverfront parks currently attract nearly one million visitors per year.

The organization is dedicated to preserving the hard work and investment it started 31 years ago and looks to expand and enhance the park system.

Contact: Tricia Theobald
Marketing and Communications Manager
Riverfront Recapture
50 Columbus Boulevard, 1st Floor
Hartford, CT 06106-1984

http://www.riverfront.org
https://www.facebook.com/riverfrontrecapture
https://twitter.com/RiverfrontRecap

Key Publishing Company

www.keypublishingcompany.com
Amazon.com
Barnes Noble.com

Jump In and Start Swimming is not only a how-to book about breaking into the lucrative field of investments but also a memoir of a second-generation-Irish American's growing-up experiences and impressive successes. It's a step-by-step tutorial from an expert and worth every penny!

Order it at KeyPublishingCompany.com and receive its accompanying *College Job and Career Guide* **free**!

James P. Naughton grew up in East Hartford, Connecticut. He graduated from Central Connecticut State University with a B.A. in English and a minor in  *psychology. He is now in the process of publishing both business and personal nonfiction books and articles (Key Publishing Company). He and his family live in North Kingstown, Rhode Island.*

www.ingramcontent.com/pod-product-compliance
Lightning Source LLC
Chambersburg PA
CBHW070527030426
42337CB00016B/2145